The Distinctive Book of
REDNECK BABY NAMES

The Distinctive Book of

REDNECK BABY NAMES

Linda Barth

Andrews and McMeel
A Universal Press Syndicate Company
Kansas City

Library of Congress Cataloging-in-Publication Data

Barth, Linda.
  The distinctive book of redneck baby names / by Linda Barth.
    p. cm.
  ISBN 0–8362–2578–3
  1. Names, Personal—Humor. 2. Rednecks—Humor. I. Title.
PN6231.N24B38 1997
818'.5407—dc21

ATTENTION: SCHOOLS AND BUSINESSES

Andrews and McMeel books are available at quantity discounts with bulk purchase for educational, business, or sales promotional use. For information, please write to: Special Sales Department, Andrews and McMeel, 4520 Main Street, Kansas City, Missouri 64111.

CONTENTS

Acknowledgments

*Special thanks to Barbara Rodriguez,
to my traveling companions Gabrielle and Carolyn,
and to Charlie, Eileen, Gary, and Jon.*

The Distinctive Book of
REDNECK BABY NAMES

INTRODUCTION

*B*abies born into redneck families need distinctive names to live up to their heritage. Somehow, the strong, safe, Anglo-Saxon names so popular today, like Ashley, Michael, or Elizabeth, seem a little too stiff, a little too formal for the wild and woolly redneck way of life.

A good redneck name is as colorful and full of music as a honky-tonk on a Saturday night. Jimmy Joe Dank. Rowena Puckett. Joe Don Mabry. Ruby Viola Cummins. Say these names out loud and you're almost singing a country ballad.

Every good redneck name tells a story. So, *The Distinctive Book of Redneck Baby Names* is much more than just a book of names; it's a book of short, short stories about each name.

Some folks may consider "redneck" a derogatory term, but those whose necks are truly red consider it a badge of honor. While redneckedness is thought to have its roots in salt-of-the-earth Southern country folk, it's actually more widespread. There are rednecks in just about every state of the Union (except maybe Connecticut), and they're not all poor and they don't all live in the sticks. There are rednecks digging in suburban gardens, running for office, and strategizing in high-stakes bass fishing tournaments. Some rednecks drive $80,000 Winnebagos, and some get by with a hot-wired '62 Chevy pickup. A unifying factor is a special language that includes unique names for unique people. In fact, names are one of the prime ways you can tell whether someone's a redneck or not. Just think about the twins Merle and Berle Blanton who married identical twin sisters named Verle and Pearl. The "Erles" all lived together in the same big house near the old cotton gin—rednecks and proud, no question. Their names all rhymed, which is one surefire way to know if someone's a redneck.

Another sign is alliteration. Say you've got a family where the parents' names are Jody and Jimmy Joe. If their kids' names are Jerry Wayne and Junelle, then look under their collars because their necks have just got to be scarlet. And any family with a male named J. D.—where the initials don't stand for anything, they're just initials—that family has automatic redneck status.

There are other ways to know if a name is a code for "redneck." Double names for boys and girls are, of course, a dead giveaway. Nicknames such as Bubba and Sally are often used as real names. Place names like Austin, Montana, and Savannah are big. Some families like to name their children after things such as cars, dolls, or nerve pills. Many girls are named after their daddies—for example, Guyette and Marvinette—but very few boys are named Sue.

If you're a redneck and want your baby to be one, too, you've got to pick the right name. It's a matter of pride in your heritage. And if you're Chip and Buffy Vandermeer with an inexplicable longing to name your baby Eula Pearle, that's okay, too, because the term "redneck" applies to a lot of people. It might even apply to you.

HOW TO KNOW IF A BABY HAS A REDNECK HERITAGE

*W*edding presents for the baby's parents included a chainsaw, a barbecue pit hand-crafted from a toxic-waste barrel, a frog gig, a carbide lamp for 'coon huntin', and a winch for the front of a pickup. And those were gifts for the bride.

The baby's family owns at least two folding aluminum lawn chairs with plastic webbing, used indoors when they're not strapped on top of the car for vacations at cousin Floyd's pig farm outside Sapps Still, Georgia.

Women in the family don't go to hairdressers or hairstylists. They go to beauty parlors. They tell the beauty parlor operator, "Rat it real high, Thelma, and don't skimp on the Aqua Net."

Too-short hosiery. Menfolk in the family wear dark, short, see-through socks that never meet the top of their pants when they sit down. The women wear knee-high hose with skirts.

The baby's bottle is filled with "Co-Cola," which the parents also drink, but from glass bottles loaded with salted peanuts, so they can swig and chomp at the same time. Big Red is served with barbecue. Pabst Blue Ribbon beer is good with breakfast.

The new baby is to be feted at a family barbecue where at least one woman shows up with pink plastic curlers in her hair.

Inside the baby's home at least one piece of taxidermy is prominently displayed in the living room. Outside, on the porch or maybe in the front yard, there's a sofa with the stuffing and springs hanging out.

The baby's noontime meal is "dinner," and as soon as he's got at least one tooth, it will include fried meat.

The family dog is named Rush, Bucky, or Elvis.

GOOD OL' BOYS AND GALS: YOUR CLASSIC REDNECK NAMES

Classic redneck names often come from Old English and Irish names. Greek and Roman names once common in the Old South are also popular with redneck families.

BOYS

CLETUS. Greek for "summoned." Cletus will get an undergraduate degree in English literature but give up on higher education when his doctoral thesis on Faulkner is rejected. The bumper sticker on Cletus's pickup will read, "My Kid Beat Up Your Honor Roll Student."

CLYDE. A Scottish name meaning "rocky eminence." And rocky is what his life will be: his wife Nonie disappearing in Vegas with no trace; that bout with lung disease after inhaling fumes at the chemical plant; his second wife running off with the plumber; his pit bull Booger biting that Snutick kid and the resulting lawsuit.

CURTIS. Old French for "courteous." Curtis's idea of courteousness is not to flirt with his wife Florine's sisters in front of Florine. When she's gone to the grocery store or beauty parlor, though, look out. Florine's sister's boy, Rusty, will bear an uncanny resemblance to his Uncle Curtis.

DALE. Old English for "valley" or "hollow." Dale will win the Waller County Cheap Heap Contest for best pickup truck held together with the most duct tape.

DARRYL. French for "beloved." Darryl's mama and aunts will spoil him rotten, and for the rest of his life he'll expect women to pamper him. A New Age redneck, he'll try to twist women's liberation to his advantage. He won't marry Rowena because, he says, marriage is enslavement of women. He will, of course, want Rowena to be the sole breadwinner while he goes drinkin' and fishin'. Call him Mr. Sensitive.

DELBERT. An old English name meaning "bright as day." He'll always be close to his mama. All the Berts will. Wilbert. Hubert. Norbert. Lambert. These are wimpy redneck names, but that happens sometimes.

DEWAYNE. Derived from the old Gaelic "Duane," this name can be spelled several ways, but "DeWayne" is preferred because you can drawl it out into two syllables. DeWayne won't make straight A's in math, but who needs the Pythagorean theorem to haul five tons of oranges from Orlando to Tucumcari in an eighteen-wheeler with customized "Keep on Truckin'" mud flaps?

DEWEY. Welsh for "prized." Your little Dewey will present you with a "prize" when he's eleven: He'll have the longest tapeworm ever removed from a child in the history of the Osceola County Free Clinic. You'll be mortified, but he'll brag about it at school, and the news will end up in Clystine Claunch's gossip column in your weekly newspaper.

DEXTER. Latin for "dexterous." Dexter will run around with that wild Wesley Deets, wear taps on his dress shoes, pouf his hair in a rockabilly pompadour, and be agile with hooks and eyes on brassieres. When he takes women into his arms for slow country dancin', he's redneck sex personified. He'll have a suave style, or at least attempt it, and that's what counts.

DWIGHT. A derivative form of "Dionysus." Oh, yeah, like Dwight could care about that. What he does care about is guns. He'll own lots of them, but his favorite will be a machine gun that he will illegally carry in his pickup truck just for fun. He'll call it "Black Beauty" and pet it sometimes.

The Country-and-Western Influence

Rednecks owe a great debt to country-and-western musicians, not only for the music, but for the names they inspire. Some rednecks become great country musicians; some musicians assume redneck names, but they're not true rednecks.

Here's a list of country-and-western musicians' names for inspiration in your quest for just the right redneck baby name. Some of the musicians below may be rednecks, some of them definitely are not, but their names have certain redneck characteristics (their first name is a classic redneck name, it's a nickname or abbreviation, it's a double name, or initials are used instead of a full name).

NAMES FOR BOYS

Chet Atkins
Clint Black
Garth Brooks
Jimmy Buffet
Johnny Cash
Billy Ray Cyrus
Jimmie Dale
    Gilmore
Merle Haggard

Ray Wiley Hubbard
    (author of the song,
    "Up Against the
    Wall, Redneck
    Mothers")
Waylon Jennings
Jerry Lee Lewis
Willie Nelson
Marty Robbins

Mel Tillis
Travis Tritt
Ernest Tubb
Porter Wagoner
Jerry Jeff Walker
Slim Whitman
Hank Williams
Dwight Yoakam
Faron Young

ELDRED. If he's like Eldred Farley, he'll sneak into his neighbor's catfish farm at night and rustle buckets full of catfish that he'll sell on the roadside during the day. He'll get caught and do six months in jail, where he'll get seriously beat up, because if there's anything lower in status at the jailhouse than a cattle thief, it's a fool catfish rustler.

EMMETT. Old German name meaning "hardworking and strong." Emmett will be a real he-man and work as a logger in Northern California. In his spare time, he'll prospect for gold in the streams of the Sierra Nevada, work as a duck-hunting guide, and moonlight as an orchard crop duster for local farmers. At age fifty-two, he'll keel over from a heart attack, leaving his widow Wanda set for life.

(See Wanda.)

ERWIN. An accomplished sausage maker, Erwin will make sausage out of beef, venison, pork, and occasionally possum and 'coon to sell at his beer joint. When a group of vegetarians moves to town and tries to open a juice bar where the Dairy Queen used to be, Erwin will perceive them as competitors. He'll put hamburger meat in their hubcaps and let the air out of their tires, snickering a little while he's doing it.

EUGENE. Redneck pronunciation: "YEW-jean." He'll always have a toothpick in his mouth and wear a hand-tooled leather belt with his name spelled out in block letters.

EUPLE. When he's thirteen, he'll rebel against his classically southern but impossibly dorky name. Euple will grow his hair long, get a bad perm, wear only torn jeans and an AC/DC T-shirt, and insist everyone call him "Billy."

FLOYD. He'll be on the same men's bowling team as Vern, Lamar, and Dwight. The name of their team will be "Four Guys with Big Balls," which Floyd's wife Mona will dutifully embroider on their bowling shirts. But the "Bowlin' Baptists" will object, so they'll have to revert to the boring shirts that read, "Vern's TV Repair."

GARLAND. Cousin of Harlan, so you know he's going to be wild. He'll join the Banditos motorcycle gang, acquire beaucoups tattoos, and change his name legally to Scum of the Earth.

GRADY. An Irish name meaning "illustrious, noble." Grady will marry that sweet Vernell Hunsucker, who'll be a great asset to him socially when he runs for county sheriff. Grady will always get reelected. One key to his popularity will be his lazy basset hound named The Deputy, who'll come to work with him, then sprawl out by his desk and sleep so soundly that visitors will ask if the dog is dead.

HARDISON. Hardison Harrison will have a rhythmic name, but that'll be the only rhythm he'll ever have. Every Sunday, he'll put on his pea-green leisure suit and lead the singin' at his local church. Using a ballpoint pen for a baton, he'll drag out the tempo of the hymns till Old Lady Riggs starts to snore. Finally, after twenty-five years, the church elders will diplomatically replace him with a younger song leader.

HARLAN. English, meaning "from the battle land." All the bullet holes in his ancient Dodge Charger were shot from the inside out.

JAMES. Somewhere in the family tree of every good redneck is a male named James. Not Jim, not Jimmy, not Jim Bob. Just James. A quiet kind of guy, he'll either be real, real smart, or dumber than a box of rocks. You never can tell with James.

LAMAR. Old German for "famous throughout the land." Lamar will be famous for his conspiracy theories. When scientists present evidence of life on Mars, Lamar will be the first to say, "I told you so." He'll grant an exclusive interview to the *Weekly World News* telling how, for years, Martians have been zapping his vital organs with laser beams.

LUTHER. German name meaning "renowned warrior." Luther will make great barbecue, his wife Lurleen will cook the beans, and they'll travel merrily all over the country in their Winnebago competing in barbecue cook-offs. Their children Lana and Larry Bob will probably always have a weight problem, as will their rat terrier Lolly, who always gets the brisket fat.

(Note: Alliteration is good. One sure sign of a redneck family is when all family members' names start with the same letter.)

LYMAN. Lyman will always be thought of as a little weird because he'll be the only redneck in America known to have a cat. Rednecks much prefer dogs, big ol' slobbery, wet-mouthed curs. If redneck men come into a little money, they'll tend to buy purebred hounds; the women will buy apricot poodles.

MERLE. Old French for "famous." Merle and his twin brother Berle will be famous, at least in Smith County, for marrying twin sisters Pearl and Verle, and they'll all live together in a big ol' house down by the cotton gin. When it comes to naming, no one can outdo rednecks for twins' names.

MONROE. An old Gaelic name, "Monroe" needs to be pronounced with the accent on the first syllable, "MON-roe," for true redneck effect.

Monroe will be plagued by dandruff his whole life long, but that won't hinder his popularity at parties because he'll be an ace-jake accordion player. His signature accordion songs will be tunes from the '70s, like "My Sharona" and "Everybody Was Kung Fu Fighting."

QUINTON. From an English place name meaning "queen's manor." Quinton and his wife Delma Lee will be hip, stylish rednecks. They'll take vacations in his restored '57 Chevy, traveling along the old Route 66 and staying in vintage motels, preferably those old Indian teepee-shaped motels made of concrete.

RODNEY. Old English name meaning "from the island clearing." Rodney and his brother J. Ray will do megabusiness selling marijuana from their bedroom when they're in their teens. They'll have lots of visitors. Their totally clueless mama will just think they're popular.

VIRGIL. Latin for "rod or staff bearer." Old Virge will carry a rod, all right—a fishing rod. Virgil will love fishing more than he loves his wife, Clovadale. That will distress her during the early years of their marriage. After about twenty years she'll realize it's a good thing.

WADE. Means "one who crosses the river." Prophetic. Wade will have a roadside snake zoo outside El Paso. When he's seventy, his first wife will die. Then his zoo manager, Sheba-the-Snake-Lady, will drug him, take him across the Rio Grande to Juarez and marry him, then knock him off and collect his $100,000 life insurance. His family will never hear from Wade again, nor will they ever find out what happened to the snakes.

WESLEY. An old English name. A dapper lady-killer, Wesley will slick back his dark, wavy hair with hair tonic and wear stiletto-pointed shoes with white lightnin' bolts on the sides. He'll finally get married at age fifty-five to Wanda Sue, sixteen, and father five children before qualifying for Social Security.

WILLARD. Old English for "bold resolve." Every time he loses at poker, Willard will vow never to gamble again, but he can't help himself. He'll work as a construction contractor, and his wife Leora will have a rule: Every time he loses $20,000, he has to redesign and redecorate their sitting room. They'll go through dozens of design schemes including Mandarin Chinese, Hawaiian tropical rattan, and an indescribable redneck version of Art Deco.

WOODROW. Means "passage in the woods" in Old English. Woodrow will be a shy, backwoods type who won't travel more than fifty miles from his home in the piney woods during his lifetime. He'll make small woodland animals like squirrels and possums his pets, and whittle replicas of them in pine. His foul-mouthed wife Venus will shrewdly market his folk art for him.

GIRLS

BERNICE. Greek for "carrier of victory." Bernice will tell every umpire who makes the wrong call in her sons' Little League games to "cram it, ram it, and rotate it." That's basically the same thing she'll tell her boys' school principal when they don't get good grades, their vocational guidance counselor, driver's ed teacher, 4-H Club adviser, and others who dare to cross her boys. Her sons will marry domineering women, and she'll constantly feud with her daughters-in-law.

BLANCHE. Means "blank" in French. Blanche will have thick ankles but enjoy a satisfying career teaching home economics in high school. She and her husband Buddy will raise two nice children.

CLYSTINE. A name combining "Clyde" and "Christine." If your daughter's like Clystine Claunch, she'll love to talk. She'll land herself a nice job writing a gossip column for the *Osceola Times*, breaking stories like who's got the biggest yellow crookneck squash in their summer garden, and who all showed up for the Sline family reunion in Rolling Fork, Mississippi.

CRYSTELL (also **KRYSTAL**). Means "clear." Which is what her mind will be—clear and uncomplicated. Her favorite thing to do on Saturday night is watch *American Gladiators*. She's secretary of the Gladiators' Fan Club and sends mushy, fawning notes to Turbo, her favorite "Glad Guy."

DARLENE. French for "little darlin'." The boys at church camp will never forget her. Your little darlin' will cut a swath through Baptist boys in five counties and be married three times before she finally settles down with DeWayne, but she'll probably always be a backslidin' Baptist.

EDNA. Hebrew for "delight." Edna will be delighted when she has her silicone breast implants removed and she collects an unmentionable, still-secret sum (rumored to be in seven figures) in her lawsuit against the silicone manufacturer. Edna will buy a condo in Vail, wear furs dyed in neon colors, and chase Eurotrash.

FERN. She'll marry Vern and go bowling twice a week for forty years. He'll build a special room for their bowling trophies.

FLORINE. Sounds very similar to "fluorine," a poisonous gas. Florine will just never understand why her husband Curtis is so indifferent to her. After all, she paints her nails dark red and wears a see-through polyester negligee every night to bed. But he's a good provider, so she puts up with him. If she notices Curtis's flirtations with her sisters, she never lets on.

FRANCINE. Variation of "Frances," meaning "free." Francine will think she lives a libertine life—she does like to have her glass of Boone's Farm Apple Wine before supper. Only problem is, she's Baptist and worries what other people think, so she'll buy her wine from a liquor store one town over. Even then, she'll drive to the "Baptist window" behind the liquor store, just in case anyone's watching.

ISOLENE. Variation on "Isolde," a mythical Irish princess. Isolene won't have a mustache till she's in her late thirties, about the same time her hips fill out real good. When she wears pantyhose and walks down the aisle at church, her plump thighs will make a mysterious swishing sound. That'll only whet J. B.'s fascination with her, but it'll take him a year to get up the nerve to ask her out because she's nineteen years older than he is.

(See J. B.)

IVALENE. Sort of a combination of "Ivy" and "Irene." In her teens, she'll like to hang out with the older guys who race at the dirt track. They'll call her "Valvoline"(sometimes "Vasoline"), and get her hooked on Camel nonfilters. She'll have a Pontiac Firebird tattooed on her butt.

JEWEL. She'll make dozens of painted plywood characters and place them on her lawn every Christmas, merrily mixing scenes of baby Jesus in the manger with cutouts of Bugs Bunny and Wilma Flintstone and other cartoon characters. Her husband Dale will string up 10,000 lights, and he and Jewel will sit outside in their lawn chairs every night the week before Christmas drinking highballs and singing Christmas carols to passersby.

JUANITA. Spanish form of "Jane." A waitress with a heart of gold, Juanita will always be a little underweight. People will tip her generously, and she and Buster will make a real nice living at their café. She'll always love Buster and see him through his many illnesses—the gout, the hemorrhoid surgery, the triple bypass, and that skin cancer that keeps growing back on the tip of his nose.

LUCILLE. Latin for "light." Lucille won't date boys from the local state university because "they're too smart."

LULU. A version of "Louise." Lulu will have a temper and throw hissy fits every now and then. You've heard the expression "a real Lulu"?

LURLEEN. German for "alluring." Lurleen's beans will be legendary on the barbecue cook-off circuit. The secret: a pinch of baking soda to take the "toot" out. Also, only use garlic salt, never fresh onions or garlic. Lurleen and Luther and their kids will smell like smoked sausage most of the time.

MAVIS. French for "thrush." Mavis will see pictures of her grandmother from the 1960s and adopt a '60s look. She'll rat her cotton-candy blonde hair real high and wear blue eye shadow, white lipstick, and miniskirts all her life.

MELBA. A form of diet toast. Melba will have a big butt, wear a hair net, work in the school lunchroom serving meals, and think she's the world's authority on nutrition. The bland food she fixes at home won't taste any better than the stuff she serves at school, but "at least it's healthy," she'll assure her family and occasional hapless dinner guests.

MERRILY. An adverb used as a name. Merrily will be a blonde cheerleader and drive the boys wild doing high kicks at football games in her white boots with tassels and short, short skirt. In tenth grade she'll fall crazy-in-love with Dexter, but her mother will forbid her to see him because he's twenty-five. Dexter will take up with an eighth-grade cheerleader and break Merrily's heart.

(See Dexter.)

M'LOU. As in "*Skip to M'.*" Also, M'Lynne. This *M*-apostrophe name connotes possession: My Lou. My Lynne. This may seem fine when she's your little girl, but what's gonna happen when she grows up and marries Willie Clyde Hubbard who's already too dang possessive to begin with? If you name her M'Lou, raise her to be headstrong and independent; she should err on the side of bitchery.

MODESTA. "Modest" in Spanish. Modesta Mooney will start seeing Jim Bob Tucker for coffee after church. After about a year, he'll ask her on a real date to his trailer house and serve TV dinners—the fancy kind—with a separate square for the apple crisp. Before they get to dessert, a loud shot will ring out, the front window will shatter, and Jim Bob will holler, "Get down! It's my wife!" Modesta will dive for the floor, and Jim Bob's estranged wife Dody will shoot out every window of the trailer house. Jim Bob will offer to drive Modesta home, but she'll walk.

MONA. A form of Old Gaelic for "noble one." Long-suffering Mona will put up with her husband Floyd's short-lived enthusiasms—the attempt at emu farming, the failed Amway products venture, the snow-cone stand franchises at stock car racetracks. Mona will hold onto her regular job at the local Pick 'n' Pack convenience store to bring in steady money.

OPHELIA. Greek name meaning "immortality." Ophelia's marriage to Luke Peters will be a happy union but an unfortunate merger of names. Adolescent pranksters will crank-call Ophelia Peters and make lewd suggestions until she and Luke give up and get an unlisted number.

OUIDA. (Pronounced o-WEED-ah). She and Hank will date for forty years in their small town, and, finally, when she retires from her job as a hardware store clerk, they'll move in together, but never marry, and nobody, not even that nosy Methodist, Loris Lou, will dare to raise a peep about their living arrangements.

ROSEANNE. After you-know-who on TV.

ROWENA. She'll weigh about 300 pounds, but Darryl will hardly notice because he's either drinkin' or fishin' with the boys. They'll have a couple of rug rats but never marry because Darryl has a problem with commitment. He can't even commit to a steady job, much less marriage. Sometimes Rowena'll get really fed up, and that's when the fireworks begin.

(See Darryl.)

SHEBA. She'll claim that seventy-year-old Wade, a snake zoo owner, died of natural causes in that Juarez motel room on their wedding night: "Way too much excitement," she'll say with a smile. She'll hide out in Juarez till Wade's insurance pays off, then catch a plane to Caracas, smuggling her favorite boa constrictor, Mephistopheles, aboard in a large basket.

VENUS. Means "goddess of love." No one will ever understand the peculiar marriage of Venus and Woodrow Spinks. They'll live in a little cabin without electricity in the woods with their seven children. Venus will raise turkeys and cuss like a sailor. Woodrow will silently whittle quirky animal figurines all day. Wearing only a cotton dress and rubber thongs, Venus will fly to New York and Washington yearly to market Woodrow's folk art, mesmerizing dealers with her husky voice and earthy language.

VERNELL. A variation of Verna, meaning "springlike." Vernell's claim to fame will be her Twinkie Jell-O salad. Lay a bunch of Twinkies out in a shallow glass dish. Mix up a box of red Jell-O and pour on top. Chill. Cut into rectangles and serve with a clean plastic spatula. On formal occasions spritz a little Redi-Whip on top. The Presbyterian Ladies Book Club, which holds fund-raisers to reelect Vernell's husband Grady as sheriff, just loves Twinkie Jell-O.

WANDA. Possibly Slavic for "woman of the Vandals." Soon after her husband Emmett's death from overwork in Northern California, Wanda will change her name to Vanessa, get a face-lift, buy a house in La Jolla, and move in her twenty-five-year-old personal trainer, Brick. They'll travel to the Mauna Kea Beach Hotel in Hawaii a lot, and she'll ditch all her friends who once knew her back in Yuba City.

ZERLENE. One of the more creative *ene* names for redneck girls. Zerlene Furr will have a hard time getting a date for the senior prom, but finally at the last minute Norbert Sourmilch will ask her, and they'll have a wonderful time.

NICKNAMES THAT ARE REAL NAMES

*R*ednecks like to keep things casual. Guys can count on one hand the times they've ever worn a necktie. Gals can count on one hand the times they've ever worn pantyhose. With such an informal lifestyle, how could anyone name a child Townsend Phipps Harrison IV? Rednecks like to name their babies nicknames, and that's what goes on the birth certificate. Billy, not William. Bessie, not Elizabeth. Call Billy "William" and he'll get mad: "If my mama'd wanted me to be called William, she would've named me William," he gripes.

BOYS

BILLY. This name works well as a double name, too (Billy Joe, Billy Bob), but some rednecks like just plain "Billy." Billy will be the best tomato gardener around. His secret: Elevate the beds in old tractor tires. Paint the tires with spray paint, and it'll make your yard look real pretty, too, he says.

Misspellings, Misunderstandings, and Disagreements

Sometimes the courthouse clerk screws up, doesn't get the name right on the birth certificate, and the child is stuck with the misspelling throughout life. Sometimes parents can't agree on what the child's name should be so they go with an interim name that stays with the child forever. And then there are parents who just flat can't spell. All these make for good redneck names.

E. E. A dyslexic courthouse clerk will write the *E*s backward on E. E. Dinkins's birth certificate. His parents will find that amusing and call him "Three Three" when he's little. When he grows up, he'll be known as Three Dinkins.

JUNE MAME's mama wrote down that her new baby girl (named for the birth month) had no middle name: "None." The nurse read it as "Mame," and that's how the courthouse recorded it.

BABEBOY WIGGINS's parents never could agree on a name, so his birth certificate reads "Baby Boy." Over the years, that evolved into Babeboy, and that's what people call him down at the domino parlor. Nobody ever teases him. He's six-foot-five and weighs 300 pounds.

LROY ERNST's name is the way his mama Leora thought you should spell "Elroy."

WANE's mama just never liked the y in Wayne.

BOBBY. Ever the inventive soul, Bobby will put a turbo-charged engine in his riding lawnmower and compete in the lawnmower division at tractor pulls. He can mow his lawn in ten minutes, too.

BUBBA. A redneck classic. Siblings in the South who can't pronounce the word "brother" say "bubba." Bubba will drive a pickup truck with a gun-rack, vote conservative, and politicians will worry over his every opinion at the state legislature. "Bubba dudn't lahk it," they'll fret. Louisiana Cajuns like to name their sons Bubba, too. Bubba Thibodeaux will sell pickup trucks in Lafayette.

BUBBER. Put the words "Bubba" and "blubber" in a blender and you get Bubber, a degenerate form of the name "Bubba." Bubber is Bubba's dumber, younger brother.

BUCK. Old English for "buck deer." And that's just what he'll hunt his whole life.

BUDDY. Sounds friendly, accessible. Buddy will be president of his fraternity. He'll eventually own an oil-tool business, eat chicken fried steaks fried only in canola oil, and wear ostrich boots with his Armani suits. Think big: "Ladies and gentlemen, the President of the United States and Mrs. Buddy Joe Feenster."

BUM. Name a son after the much-beloved former Houston Oilers coach, Bum Phillips, and he'll have football in his blood. He'll have good manners, too, just like Bum, who refused to wear his cowboy hat in the Astrodome during games because his mama told him it wasn't polite to wear a hat indoors.

BUSTER. If he's anything like your cousin Buster Binge, he'll marry that stringy-haired Juanita Ferkle straight out of high school and become a short-order cook while she waits tables. He'll put on a couple hundred pounds, get gout and heart disease, and finally lose weight by learning to bake foods that taste fried, à la Oprah Winfrey and Paul Prudhomme. His friends in heart attack rehab will swarm the Buster Binge Cafe.

CHICK. Sure, "Chick" may not seem like a manly redneck name, but if you've ever seen the awesome Chick McCleod ride his trained longhorn steer into the town square, tie it to a tree, and walk into the Coleto Creek Saloon for a jigger or two of George Dickel sourmash, you'd reconsider.

DOC. You've heard the expression, "Never eat at a cafe called 'Mom's,' never play poker with a man named 'Doc,' and never sleep with someone who has more troubles than you"? Well, Doc will put himself through college playing Bourre, a Cajun form of poker.

DUDE. There is such a thing as a redneck surfer, especially along the Gulf Coast of the Florida panhandle, which is known as the Redneck Riviera. The waves aren't nearly as high as those in California or Hawaii, but that won't bother Dude Jenkins, as long as he's got his Jimmy Buffet tunes and a cooler full of Shiner Bock beer.

FOB. After Fob James, governor of Alabama. Guys named Fob sound like they come from old southern families and old southern money, even if they don't. Fob Grimes, for example, all buffed, tanned, and muscular, looks like a hero straight out of a southern bodice-ripper. He'll deliver packages for UPS, and sometimes women will send packages to themselves via UPS just so they can see Fob.

FRICK. A variation of "Frederick." Frick will think he can fix any electrical appliance—even toasters—with a bent coat hanger.

HECK. Short for "Hector." Should you really name your child a name that sounds like a mild oath? Heck, yeah. Heck Hodie will be a successful real-estate agent selling farmettes and rancheritos to suburban rednecks who've had to move from the farm to the city to make a living yet still want a few acres to farm. (The "expatriates," he calls 'em.) Heck'll take stuffed deer hooves and "tump" 'em into the ground to make hoof prints on the ranch he's about to sell. Then he'll point out the hoof prints to potential buyers and tell them the land is plentiful with wildlife.

JOJO. Cute version of "Joseph," which means "Jehovah adds." Does He ever. Jojo will work as a toolpusher on an oil rig in Algeria, spending two weeks a month there, then two weeks in Pansey, Alabama, where he'll have plenty of idle time to get into buttloads of trouble with women. Jojo will be married eight times and have twelve kids.

JUNIOR. Not Jim Bob Tucker Jr. Not Hardison Harrison Jr. Just Junior. That's his legal name. Junior will be rich by some folks' standards because he'll own five cars. Problem is, none of 'em will run, but that won't matter a whole heck of a lot because Junior ain't goin' nowhere.

LINK. Short for "Lincoln." Also, a verb meaning "to connect." Link will be a great running back for his high school football team. One day after football practice, he and that teenaged vixen Lova Lee Fields will proceed to "make out" under the bleachers, and Mrs. Feenster, the home ec teacher, will see them and tattle to his parents. Link will be shipped off to military school in Virginia. Twenty-five years later, after a couple of marriages each, Link and Lova Lee will finally connect, marry, and live happily ever after.

LUKE. Men named Luke like to wear vests. Luke Peters will be a champion pancake flipper at Knights of Columbus fund-raising pancake suppers. He and his wife Ophelia will be great country swing dancers, too.

MACK. Irish or Gaelic for "son of." His wife will call him "Mack-a-bitch" when she's mad. He'll drive—what else?—a Mack truck and be away from home a lot.

MONK. When Monk goes gray, he'll secretly die his chest hair with Grecian Formula so he can still wear his cowboy shirts unbuttoned almost to the navel when he goes honky tonkin'. Even when he's ninety he'll dance like he's sixteen, and women will wait in line to dance with him.

NEWT. After Speaker of the House Newt Gingrich. If you name a kid "Newt," expect him to be tough as nails. The name works well for pit bulls, too.

NORM. Norm's always going to be a little hefty and have trouble covering up his butt crack with blue jeans when he bends over. Sometimes even when he's standing upright. But he won't care.

PREACHER. A popular first name in Tennessee. Preacher will be wild as a March hare while growing up, then true to his name, take to preaching the gospel when he's older, not unlike Billy Graham's son.

RANDY. Almost every Randy on Earth will have a rebellious phase. Randy Fudge will run an illegal methamphetamine lab in the cactus and mesquite country outside Alice, Texas. One morning, he'll wake up and see eight

Texas Rangers with bloodhounds surrounding his shack. Nuttily enough, he'll try to make a run for it. He'll drench his sneakers with Clorox to throw the dogs off his scent, then bust out the front door and run like hell toward a mesquite thicket. The Rangers will pepper his butt with buckshot and haul him in.

RED. A snazzy dresser, he'll have red hair and a red goatee and wear two-toned white and brown "correspondent" shoes, the kind of shoes a correspondent in a divorce case would have been expected to wear in the days when fault had to be proven in divorce. Red will have a penchant for married women and be the primo, number one cause of a lot of divorces.

RUSTY. He'll be a defense lawyer and wear fancy lizard-skin boots. His fellow rednecks will despise him for his livelihood—until they need him, of course, for defense against charges such as DWIs, aggravated assaults, and paternity suits. Then he'll be their best friend (and chief creditor).

SHORTY. Cruising the main drag of DeRidder, Louisiana, on a Saturday night with the guys, Shorty will be the backseat bartender. The guys will favor Shorty's Instant Margarita (lime Slurpee with tequila). For the ladies they convince to come riding with them, he'll mix Shorty's Red Menace (Big Red soda water with Everclear).

SMILEY. He'll abhor and avoid yuppie food at all costs, especially portobello mushrooms and cilantro.

SNOOKY. Anyone named "Snooky" is going to love TV. Snooky Stubbs will take his electric generator, portable Sony, and small satellite dish with him to his deer blind.

SNUFF. Short for "Snuffy." Snuff will be lean and wiry and call square dances, pausing occasionally to spit the juice from his wad of Skoal into a little pewter spittoon six feet away.

SONNY. He'll sell insurance for a while but neglect to send people's premiums to the home office because he's used their money to bet at the dog track. Just a little loan to himself, y'know. So he may have to do a little time behind bars, but he will have learned his lesson and be okay.

TROY. Or Trey. Means "the third." If you're Billy Joe Simper Jr., then your son can be Billy Joe Simper III, and you can call him Troy, or Trey, for short. Some people name their boys "Troy" without realizing it's a number thing, though. Troy will name his son Cuatro. The line of progression will continue through Cinco and Seis until Siete, when the line will die out, and the family will have to start all over again with a new name.

VERN. Short for "Vernon," which means "springlike, youthful" in Latin. Vern will be thin and wiry and think he's the world's expert on everything. He'll fix TVs for a living and bore everyone at barbecues talking about the difficulties of installing the new cathode tube in Roy Bob's dang-fool giant-screen TV. Just before the Super Bowl, however, Vern will be everyone's best friend.

WES. With his shoulder-length black hair and totally tattooed upper body, Wes will fancy himself a warlock. Strange bonfires and weird chanting at night on his farm will spook the neighbors. He'll have business cards printed up that read, "Wes the Warlock." Parents won't let their kids play with Wes and Lottie's kids after school.

GIRLS

ANNIE. Redneck women are never named Ann, always Annie. If your Annie is like Annie Shomp, she'll be addicted to the Home Shopping Network and order tons of jewelry made with Cubic Zirconia.

AZALIE. The name is derived from "azalea" but pronounced "AZ-a-lee," sorta like "Merrily." Azalie Cottle will keep a flock of chickens in her backyard and sell the eggs for pin money. She'll give each hen a name and talk real sweetly to it when taking its eggs.

BABY. Her mama will be so exhausted after giving birth to her, she'll name her the first thing that comes into her mind: Baby. When Baby grows up, she'll have a passel of nieces and nephews and they'll all call her Aunt Baby.

Beauty Parlor Operator Names

Rednecks know that if you really want to find out what's going on in a town, you don't go to the newspaper editor or to the police department or the county courthouse, you go to the beauty parlor. Not to a hair salon, not to a beauty boutique—to a genuine beauty parlor where they still put women's hair in rollers and make 'em sit under a hair dryer.

While they're rolling and ratting everyone's hair, beauty parlor operators are gathering information that they will (no doubt) share with others, perhaps for years to come. They not only know who's getting a divorce, they know exactly why. They know whose child is sick and who can't make their mortgage this month. Now if the person who does your hair is named Biffy, you're probably not going to get good gossip from her stiff little pursed lips. But if you go to a beauty parlor and any of the operators have the following names, you can be pretty sure it's a redneck beauty parlor and they'll talk your ears off: Florence, Lucille, Opal, and Irma. If you name your daughter after any of these women, at least you know she'll always be able to make a living doing people's hair. And you'll always know what's going on around town.

BESSIE. An addictive personality, Bessie will quit smoking but get hooked on nicotine gum, nasal spray, over-the-counter cough syrup, and sinus tablets. Every Sunday at church, when the preacher issues the call for all sinners to get right with God, Bessie will walk down the aisle, lay her drugs on the altar, and cry and plead for forgiveness, promising never to take them again. Her weekly confessions will start to get on the nerves of certain staid church ladies, who notice that Bessie always seems to take her drugs home with her after the service.

BONZIE. She and her twin Bonnie will have a knack for art and make concrete figurines like angels and gargoyles for permanent lawn decorations. Their two favorite words they'll use to describe their art are "precious" and "darlin'." Most of their money, though, will come from the pink plastic flamingoes they sell on the side.

CONNIE. From Constance, meaning "constant, firm." What a flirt. She'll wear false eyelashes, Lee Press-On Nails, and a Wonderbra—in eighth grade! Always ahead of the curve, she'll ask Jerry Wayne Payne to marry her in ninth grade. They'll wait a couple of years before making it legal. Townspeople will scoff, but she and Jerry Wayne will show them: They'll be married sixty-two years.

DEEDEE. A variation of "Diana," Latin for "divine." DeeDee will marry Sherman, her high school math teacher the day after she graduates, causing quite a scandal. It'll last about twenty years, and then old Sherm will find another high school girl to marry, leaving DeeDee really P.O.'ed. She'll take up with the Thompson boy, who's a ripe twenty-three, for revenge.

DODY. After Jim Bob asks for a divorce, she'll vow to make his life miserable, and boy, will she. She'll shoot out the windows of his trailer house, slash his tires several times, order thirty pizzas sent to his house C.O.D., and call the electric company and have his electricity cut off for Christmas. Oh, and she'll kidnap his old, yeller dog Soozy and have the vet put her to sleep. Don't mess with Dody.

EFFIE. She'll be six feet tall and a mean drunk. In high school, she'll break a beer bottle over Johnnyboy Edwards's head at a picnic, he'll have to have twenty stitches, and she'll be temporarily suspended from the basketball team. Most of the time, though, she'll be clean and sober and the sweetest thing on Earth. A great quilter, with those long fingers.

FLOSSIE. A variation of "Florence." Flossie will have a flair for the exotic. When widowed in her sixties, she'll regularly attend her Assembly of God church's "Gospel Gong Show," a talent night for singles. One night she'll win with her "Castanets for Christ" routine, dancing with castanets to Ravel's *Bolero* while wearing a homemade gypsy costume.

JODY. The ultimate cowgirl. She'll have a living room full of barrel-racing trophies and marry Jerry Jack Jones, a farrier who'll keep her horses well shod. She'll breed quarter horses, Angus cattle, Catahoula Leopard pups, and, sometimes, Jerry Jack.

LIBBY. Her boyfriend Hank won't look like much, and he'll pick his nose in public and spit at inappropriate times and in inappropriate places, but Libby will think he hung the moon and marry him. She'll tell anyone who'll listen, "I'm so-o-o lucky to have him." Behind her back, her women friends will cattily refer to her beloved as "Mucous Man."

LILLIE. Like the flower. She'll have a flawless complexion without wrinkles all her life. Her beauty secret she'll never divulge? Crisco—rednecks' all-purpose grease. Instead of cold cream, rub a thin film of Crisco on your face and neck.

MARGE. She'll sing tenor in her women's barbershop quartet group, Large Marge and the Margarines.

MINNIE. After Dickie Lee leaves her for that tube-topped hussy he met at the tractor pull, mousy little Minnie will take up weight training and be named Ms. Olympia in a national female bodybuilding contest.

NELLIE. Nickname for "Helen," Greek for "torch" or "light." Nellie and her husband Fred, who runs a feed store, will win a trip to Paris, along with a bunch of other American feed store owners. Once they get there, Nellie will decide she doesn't like it and want to return home. The nongroup airfare to return to the good ol' U.S. of A. will be $3,000, so they'll decide to tough it out in Paris for a week. Nellie won't ever really find anything she likes to eat, and when shopping she'll find the clothes "trashy."

NONIE. Nonie will be a simpy little brown wren who marries at age fifteen and takes heaps of verbal abuse from creepy Clyde, her husband. One day they'll take a road trip to Vegas, she'll disappear in Harrah's, and he'll never see her again. Five years later, he'll return to Vegas and notice a chorus dancer who looks vaguely familiar, but he'll be too stupid to figure it out.

OUISIE. Pronounced "Weezie." A version of "Louise." She'll move to town to be a teacher, and one day, on the porch of the old country store, she'll meet and fall instantly in love with that cute J. W. Supple, a pig farmer. Six months later they'll be married on the porch in a tailgate wedding with all J. W.'s friends circled 'round in their pickups, drinkin' beer, and hollerin', "Don't do it, J. W.!"

PENNY. Short for "Penelope," which probably means "weaver" in Greek, not that anybody in Penny's hometown of Two Egg, Florida, would give a flip. Penny's husband, Mervin, will have mysterious ailments and won't be able to work, so she'll set up a little hamburger stand off Interstate 10 near

Tallahassee, and with her two little Bunsen burners and a fry griddle, sell burgers and raise a family of four nice kids.

PINKY. She'll have pale white skin and strawberry blonde hair and have to take asthma medication. Living near a toxic waste dump won't help her allergies, but no one will ever be able to convince her to move.

RITA. Short for "Margarita," her mother's favorite cocktail at the Hush Honey Hush lounge (but only before pregnancy, never during).

SALLY. A variation of the name "Sarah," which is Hebrew for "princess." Long, tall Sally will smoke long, brown More cigarettes, tan her face to a leathery brown, cuss like a sumbitch, and win national skeet shooting championships. Her husband and three sons will adore her.

SANDY. From "Sandra," which is Greek for "defender of mankind." Perfect, 'cuz she's gonna be a blonde cheerleader. She'll marry Joe Roy Stuckey, who'll become a coach, and she'll teach Sunday School at the Methodist Church in Waycross, Georgia. Joe Roy will be enamored of her, stretch marks and all, her whole life long.

SISSY. The female equivalent of "Bubba." It's what siblings in the South sometimes call their sister. Sissy will be a tomboy with braids and braces and be the best softball pitcher in five counties. She might settle down with Jim Ed Blanton and have a passel of kids and coach girls' softball. Or, she might run away with Rowena to Eureka, California, where they'll start a furniture refinishing business together. Hard to tell about Sissy.

SUNNY. She'll drive a Caterpillar tractor, doing road construction work to support her no-'count husband Johnny Ray Gray. Johnny Ray will drink her paycheck away, so she won't have money to get her front tooth fixed when a piece of gravel knocks it out.

SUZIE. Sometimes known as "Suzie Q." When Garland "Scum of the Earth" Sanders won't marry her after knocking her up, Suzie will join the Children of God commune outside Gallup, New Mexico, and live in a yurt where she'll deliver her son Marlon. She'll change her name to Loiyetu, a Miwok Indian name meaning "farewell to spring in bloom." They'll live happily in the commune for about fourteen years, until Marlon up and joins his dad's motorcycle gang.

TAMMY. British feminine form of "Thomas." If you're feeling kind of fancy, you'll want to name her Tamara—but call her Tammy for short. Tammy will be a sweet, faithful Christian but have big-time problems with her love life. Tammy Faye Baker. Tammy Wynette.

VICKIE. Certain nicknames can be a variation of the family's surname. This is good for redneck families with rhythm: Vickie Vick. Becky Beck, Allie Allen.

DOUBLE NAMES

$\mathcal{T}$he child's so nice they name it twice. Why do rednecks do that? Maybe it's because double names seem more important and have more weight when they're longer. Maybe it's just a rhythm thing. The names Jim and Ed are plain, but put 'em together—Jim Ed Booker—and you've got some mojo working. Double names often use two nicknames together for a doubly friendly tone.

BOYS

BILLY BOB. The night club in Ft. Worth gives this name its cachet, as does writer/actor/film director Billy Bob Thornton.

BILLY JACK. Like the movie character, he'll know karate moves and mix Eastern mysticism with violence.

BILLY JOE. He'll grow up to be a great big good ol' boy, six-foot-three and 240 pounds. He'll make good money as a roughneck in the oil patch, but he'll have a little secret: He's afraid of the dark and can't work the night shift.

BOB JAMES. He'll get religion and handle snakes at tent-show revival meetings. He'll only be bitten once, by a rattlesnake he startles when taking it out of the box. The Lord will let him live, and he'll give a moving testimony afterward about the power of faith.

BRODON. Short for "Brother Don." "Brother" is often used instead of "mister" in the South when addressing older members of your church. You can shorten this honorific to "bro" and work it into any number of names. Brobob. Brojohn. Brojim.

DANLEE. The use of "Dan" as an adverb. Rhymes with "manly."

DICKIE LEE. An ace-jake mechanic, he'll rev up his tractor, paint it bright yellow, and begin to win big-time tractor pulls. But with fame and fortune will come heartbreak. He'll leave his mousy wife Minnie for Fawn Simper, the Miss Kentucky Tractor Pull runner-up, 1995. After about a year, Fawn will leave him for a farmer with a bigger, louder tractor.

DON ROY. If he'd work in a legitimate business, he'd be a millionaire, but no, he has to run scams. When not in jail, he'll start up a weight-loss clinic somewhere, hang up a fake diploma, and charge fat women $100 for counseling and placebo diet pills. He'll sleep with his clients, then talk them into loaning him money to start up a flower shop, a magazine, a restaurant, whatever. He'll become engaged to five of his women investors simultaneously, then get hauled back to jail before he has to say, "I do."

DORWAYNE. Pronounced "DOOR-wayne." This name is one of the rare instances where a male gets to be named after his mama. Partially, anyway. Dorwayne is a combination of his parents' names, Doris and DeWayne. Of course, Doris and DeWayne won't be married to each other (DeWayne and Darlene are married for life), but that'll never bother Doris as long as DeWayne's child-support checks keep coming.

EDDIE JOE. He'll eat green onions dipped in mustard at almost every meal, sing Buddy Holly songs, and be founding editor of an oil industry trade magazine called *Lubrication Monthly*.

GARY DON. As soon as he can shake the dirt from Cowpens, South Carolina, off his young and tender feet, he'll head north to New York City and become an art director for a men's fashion magazine. He won't deny his southern upbringing, but he will drop the "Don" from his name. He'll give wonderful parties at his Fire Island beach house where he'll serve black-eyed peas, hush puppies, and champagne.

Closet Rednecks

You see them in boardrooms and architects' offices and universities all over America, but you can't tell they've got redneck names because they've moved far away from home and changed their names. They never attend high school reunions. William J. Harrison IV was Billy Joe Harrison in high school. Liza Lou Crump married a Yankee named Parker Knowles Danforth and now goes by the name Elizabeth Danforth.

A general rule of thumb: When they get a little raise or are promoted in their jobs, rednecks sometimes drop the second name; Billy Joe becomes Billy. If it's a really good promotion, he becomes Bill. If it seems they're grooming him for president of the company, he becomes William J. Harrison IV. A true redneck, of course, would stay Billy Joe Harrison to the end of his days, come what may.

JERRY WAYNE. Don't worry that "Wayne" is a common middle name for serial killers—your Jerry Wayne will be a successful shoe salesman who always convinces his buddies to buy a white belt to go with their white patent leather dress shoes. He'll get a good commission on odor-eater shoe cushions, too.

JIM BOB. You could name him James Robert, but then it wouldn't be as short and snappy and friendly, would it? Jim Bob will run a feed store and host a weekly domino game after hours.

JIMMY DEAN. Should you name your son after a sausage? Jimmy Dean Furlock's mama thinks so.

JIMMY JOE. He'll know how to make a meal stretch to feed lots of people. Jimmy Joe Dank, for instance, is the oldest in a family of ten kids. Sometimes they'll make what's known as Dank gravy and have gravy-bread for supper. Jimmy Joe's mama, Junelle, will mix up flour and old bacon grease in the skillet while he milks the cow in the yard till it puts out every drop it can. Then he'll add the milk to the skillet and if that isn't enough, he'll add water to thin it out. Each child gets a piece of white bread and a ladle of gravy. It's right tasty.
(See Junelle.)

JOE BOB. The names Joe or Bob make great middle names, too, sorta like grace notes. Eddie Joe. Billy Bob. Joe Bob reviews drive-in movies. Joe Bob Briggs.

JOE DON. Name a kid Joe Don and he's almost guaranteed to be smart and handsome. Joe Don's maiden aunt Ruby Viola will put him through medical school, and he'll repay her with a nice new house, complete with a little dog run for her Chihuahuas. Dr. Joe Don Cummins will buy a ranch and raise purebred Hereford cattle, delivering calves with as much care as he delivers babies.

JOE WILLIE. When he comes into money, he'll drop the "Willie." If he comes into a whole lotta money and his wife has serious social pretensions, he'll change his name to Joseph W. Worthington III.

JOHNNIE BOB. He'll wear wild butterfly- and floral-print boxer shorts that you can see underneath his thin, seersucker dress slacks. This will serve as a constant source of amusement to his snickering students in sixth-grade music appreciation class.

JOHNNY RAY. His wife Sunny will be the sunshine of his life, but even she won't be able to keep him away from the bottle (actually, the beer can). When drinking at the Buckhorn Bar, he'll crush beer cans slightly to fit his hand so they don't slip when he lifts them to his mouth.

MACK ED. He'll have a "TCB" ring specially made up with diamonds in homage to Elvis, whose "Taking Care of Business" logo with lightning bolt has become an insider cult symbol for fans of the King.

RAY BOYCE. Sounds almost like "Ray-boy" but not quite. Ray Boyce will be a redneck bookie specializing in bets on college football and basketball games. He'll be a dapper dresser and have a racy, pencil-thin mustache.

RICKEY RAY. After the convict in Arkansas who, before he was executed, couldn't finish the dessert of his last meal and asked to save it "for later."

ROY JOE. Or Joe Roy. Does it matter? He'll go to college on a football scholarship, blow out a knee, then run a gas station and, as a sideline, become a bookie on pro games. Some years will be luckier than others.

SAM GUS. This blue-eyed, baby-faced boy will grow up to be so handsome, people will hardly notice his weird double name. He'll become an advertising account executive for a smokeless tobacco product.

SAM TOM. He'll live in a double-wide mobile home that has a big porch where he'll sit all day practicing casting with his rod and reel. He won't talk to anybody passing by; he'll just keep casting his fishing line out into the yard, over and over, like he thinks he's going to catch a worm or something.

TOMMY LEE. He'll be dark and brooding, like the characters that actor Tommy Lee Jones plays in the movies. Tommy Lee Akins's mama, Loretta, will name her son Tommy Lee after watching *Natural Born Killers* about fifteen times.

WARD WAYNE. Alliteration is always fun. Just try to say Ward Wayne Warwas's full name after downing a six-pack. Ward Wayne will farm cotton yet wear polyester slacks to town. Go figure.

WILLIE CLYDE. When told by the doctor that he has bipolar disease, he'll think that means he's contracted a social disease from two Eskimos.

WILLIE LEE. He'll win a $20 million state lottery, buy a bass boat, take off with his wife Willene, and never be heard from again. (Don't tell anyone, but actually they'll move to Florida where it's impolite to ask, "What do you do for a living?")

GIRLS

ALICE PEARL. She'll have red hair, be a union organizer for petrochemical workers, and own 2,000 books. A liberal redneck, she'll vote "yellow-dog Democrat" every election of her life.

ALMA JEAN. Her redneck enchiladas, with the tortillas dipped in chili powder grease so they're bright red, will make her rich and famous. Well, semi-famous, anyway, at her café in the piney woods of East Texas.

BERTHA SUE. She'll weigh ninety-five pounds and always keep a lit Marlboro dangling from her lips, even as she serves up platters of fried chicken at the Lucky Leghorn Inn. Whenever anyone asks for extra cream gravy, she'll go back into the kitchen, grumbling quietly about certain "lard butt" customers as she ladles the gravy into a little bowl, letting little flecks of cigarette ash drift into the cream gravy so it looks like pepper.

BETTY JETTY. She'll have an identical twin sister named Jetty Betty. Their whole lives long, they'll never let anyone shorten their names. When you see them walking down the street together, you can't just say, "Oh, here comes Betty and Jetty." No, you have to say, "Well, hello, Betty Jetty and Jetty Betty," or they'll get mad.

BETTY JO. From the British "Elizabeth," which is what she'll change her name to in college. She'll become third-chair violin in the New York Philharmonic Orchestra, and everybody at the Dairy Queen back home will be so proud. "That Betty Jo, she's quite a fiddler," they'll say. "She's with the New York Philharmonica, you know."

BEULAH PEARL. Her friends will call her "Pearl" out of mercy.

DARLA SUE. She and her husband J. Ray Flatt will travel with their grandkids to Graceland in what has become for some families a classic pilgrimage to "redneck Mecca." They'll even stay in the motel next door to Graceland where there's a guitar-shaped swimming pool and Elvis movies on TV around the clock. They'll visit Graceland all day, then stop at the Elvis mall nearby and nudge Japanese tourists out of the way to buy guitar-shaped flyswatters to take back to the folks in Walla Walla, Washington.

DELMA LEE. She'll travel the world with Quinton, mesmerizing everyone with her charm, sense of humor, and endless collection of chiffon scarves from the 1950s.

DOE RAE. Everyone will expect her to be a music teacher but she'll have a tin ear.

DORALEE. Like the role of the secretary that Dolly Parton played in *9 to 5*, Doralee will start out working for an abusive boss and end up running the company.

GRACIE MAE. She and her husband Heck Hodie's favorite wedding present will be a videotape of the TV miniseries *Lonesome Dove*, which they'll keep on top of the coffee table, right next to the family Bible.

JUNELLE. A combination of June and Ella. She'll marry that darlin' Damon Dank and have ten kids just like that, wham, wham, wham, before she even knows what hit her. They'll all get by on white bread and watered-down cream gravy also known as Dank gravy by folks who come to visit. There'll be some concern about scurvy in the family, but a basket of oranges from the county social worker will fix that.

(See Jimmy Joe.)

KAY FAY. Remember, if it rhymes, it's almost certain to be redneck. Kay Fay will have a flair for art and paint hundreds of pictures of Elvis on black velvet. Unfortunately, she won't have a flair for business, and she'll have to pay a few thousand dollars in a lawsuit settlement for selling her velvet Elvis paintings without permission from the Presley estate.

LARUE LAVERLE. Choose this name for your little girl only if you're a stage mother like Connie McCracken. Connie wanted only the best for her little girl, so she gave her the fanciest name she could think of and started entering her baby in beauty contests. By the time LaRue LaVerle was thirteen, she'd been in more than 200 beauty contests. LaRue LaVerle got married at sixteen, had a little girl at seventeen, and started entering that baby in beauty contests, much to Connie's delight.

LETA RUTH. Leta Ruth Pugh won't like to crochet, quilt, read novels, or cook. She won't drink or dance, either. So she'll just form a club of her lady friends called The Do-Nothin' Club. They'll get together and sit in the aluminum lawn chairs on her front porch and just do nothin' once a week for a whole afternoon while the world passes them by.

LETHA FAY and **LONDA RAE.** If you name your daughter after either of the Leathers sisters, expect big trouble. Tattoos, nude Jell-O wrestling, cocaine rehab—you name it, they've been there, done that. They'd sneak into honky-tonks in junior high, passing themselves off as eighteen-year-olds, and they must've spent a fortune in eye makeup and Summer Blonde hair lightener. They became exotic dancers, then married and settled down later, but in their prime they were, um, legendary.

LORIS LOU. Her dresses may have puffy sleeves and lots of lace, but nobody much falls for her "sweet" routine. One day at her sewing circle, nosy Loris Lou will start a rumor that the Hayes girl, who's thirteen, and John Ed Smoot, fourteen, are "gettin' way too serious." The rumor will get back to the girl's mama, who'll threaten to sue Loris Lou for slander.

LOU JEAN. She and her husband Lester, a lawn-turf farmer, will get invited to the governor's inaugural luncheon because of their generous political contributions. Lou Jean will think it's the best food she ever ate and go around asking others, "You're not gonna eat that? Well, can I have it?" She'll take home a big sack of leftovers for her dogs, too.

LOU PEARL. "Lou" is a shortened feminine form of the name "Louis." "Pearl" is a gem from an oyster. Any name starting with Lou is good. Lou May, Louetta, Lou Ada. Lou Pearl sounds best, though. Lou Pearl will become a telephone operator and survive the company's downsizing.

LOVA LEE. Say it real fast and it sounds like "lovely." Never one to be a cheerleader, Lova Lee's more the type to be making out under the bleachers than leading the crowd out front.
    (See Link.)

MARY LETTA. Certain crude jokesters will say that she and her sister Fannie Mae's last name should've been "Fart."

MARY RALPH. Mary, all alone, is just too plain for rednecks. You gotta have a little extra spunk. Add a boy's name, and you've got an interesting mixture. Also, Mary Lou, Mary Beth, Mary Jo, Mary Blanche, Mary Nell.

NELDA JUNE. She'll take full advantage of the "four-fer" happy hour special every night at the Chip Kicker Lounge—four drinks for the price of one.

ROJEAN. The name's a combination of "Rolonda" (from the TV show) and "Jean." RoJean Butts will wear duct tape for a brassiere, chew Red Man chewing tobacco, and spend a couple of years on the women's wrestling circuit. She'll steal watermelons from her neighbors' patch, but they'll be so scared of her they won't say anything.

RUBY VIOLA. Her name sounds like a red musical instrument. Sweet Ruby Viola Cummins will keep about a dozen inbred Chihuahua dogs as pets. Never one to master the Spanish language, she'll call them "Chi-wow-wows." At Christmas she'll sew little red-plaid ruffled dog collars for them and take the dogs over to the local nursing home to entertain everyone.

TINY BELL. If she's anything like Tiny Bell Watkins, she'll be lucky at bingo, which she'll play down at the church parish hall every Monday and Thursday afternoon.

VONA MAE. She'll have *The Shining* on videocassette and tell people's fortunes. Sometimes she'll do seances. One night, with Jim Bob Swindle and seven other people gathered around her candlelit dining room table, the ghost of Judd Jones will appear and accuse Jim Bob of murdering him. Jim Bob will flop over dead of a heart attack at the table. No one will ever believe this story except the seven people left alive to tell it.

INITIALS

*R*ednecks love to use initials instead of full names. Sometimes the initials stand for something. Sometimes they don't. Males are more likely to use initials than females. Sometimes initials are used to cover up a really peculiar name like Edgar Erastus, and sometimes they just sound more musical. C. Ray Gooch sounds so much better to the ear than just Ray Gooch. Initials can stand all alone, or be mixed with a first or second name. They look good stamped on the back of a leather belt. And they can sound so executive like, too: J. R., J. P., R. J. One thing's for sure, though: If you've got somebody named J. D. in your family, you are definitely a redneck.

BOYS

B. JOE. Sounds like a command. B. Joe McElroy has more rhythm and sounds more assertive than Billy Joe McElroy, which is what his name will be before he gets older and tougher.

C. J. Like all good rednecks, he'll prefer Heinz 57 ketchup—lots of it—on every meat dish ever served to him.

DUB. Short for the initial *W.* Short, efficient, to the point. Also, very upscale redneck. Dub will rise above his humble beginnings in Soddy-Daisy, Tennessee, get a scholarship to Harvard, and fit right in with Biff, Todd, and Chad. Then he'll move to Louisville and become a bank president.

E. F. Only his wife and his deceased mama and daddy know what these initials stand for, and E. F. ain't tellin' anybody else.

F. M. Like the radio band-width that some "progressive" country music stations broadcast on. Name your kid F. M. and expect him to be about half-hippy. Deep rednecks don't know jack about FM radio; they only have AM in their '62 Chevy pickups.

H. E. H. E. and his brother W. E. will be called "He" and "We" growing up.

I. C. Sounds kind of mystical, like "I see." I. C. will have the uncanny ability to predict the sex of babies before they're born. He'll also be able to cure babies of thrush using a secret little trick he'll learn from his Grandma Nonie.

J. B. An insecure Mama's boy, he'll marry Isolene, a woman twice his age with as much facial hair as he has. They'll be very, very close.

J. D. A crucial litmus test for redneckedness, these are classic redneck initials. They shouldn't stand for anything, just J. D. Any family with a male named J. D. is—automatically and forever—redneck.

J. R. As in J. R. Ewing of the *Dallas* TV series, upscale redneckism at its finest.

J. RAY. He'll have sideburns and resemble the older, fatter Elvis. When he and Darla Sue and the grandkids make their pilgrimage to Graceland, J. Ray will get up early in the morning to make the thirty-minute free visit to Elvis's grave before the gates officially open. He'll sit alone by the grave, contemplating the similarities in his and Elvis's lives—the ups and downs, the tragedies and triumphs—and quietly shed a tear or two.

J. W. Stands for Johnny Walker. This'd work well if your last name's "Black."

L. C. Sounds like "Elsie," but L. C. will be confident of his masculinity and be able to deal with it.

L. L. L. L. Suggs will have the same first initials as L. L. Bean, founder of the famed mail-order retail company in Maine. L.L. Bean's clothing and outdoor gear are preppy; L. L. Suggs is definitely not, so having the same first initials will be the only thing these two L. L.s have in common.

MICKEY D. Never just Mickey. Always Mickey D. He'll be a sensitive undertaker who doesn't understand why most morticians want to send rednecks into eternity wearing neckties when they never wore them in their earthly life. No sirree, Micky D.'s rednecks are gonna be comfortable forever when he buries them in their John Deere caps, Dickies work pants, and plain cotton T-shirts with red suspenders. If they want to go to their great reward in hunters' camouflage and a shotgun across their chest, he can arrange that, too.

N. H. Some people might think these initials stand for "New Hampshire," but N. H. will never travel north of Interstate 10 in his entire life, so he won't know or care what the initials mean.

O. A. Sounds a little like "away." He'll grow into this name even more as he gets older and more forgetful.

O. D. Popular initials for a name, even if they do connote "drug overdose" in some baby-boomer rednecks' minds.

P. L. He goes by these initials because his full name is Peyton Luther Ferguson.

R. F. In his divorce settlement with Royce Ann, he'll give up custody of the kids in exchange for getting to keep the chainsaw and backhoe he and Royce Ann got as wedding gifts.

T. D. Popular initials for a boy, as they connote success on the gridiron—touchdown!

'TIT CARL. Very Cajun. Pronounced "Tee Carl" or "Teet Carl." The *'Tit* is short for the French word *petit*, which means "little." *'Tit* is like the *ie* diminutive at the end of names, so "'Tit Carl" is sort of the Cajun version of "Carlie." Sometimes Cajuns just use the initial *T.*, so it'd be "T. Carl." Sometimes they use a *T*-apostrophe, as in "T'Carl." If you meet someone named 'Tit John, T. Tommy or T'Man, he's a Cajun good ol' boy.

TUFFY J. He'll organize a 'Coon Hunt for Christ to raise money for a new church building, just like that church in Alabama did several years ago. Only problem is, Tuffy J. will take about three-fourths of the money that should've gone to Jesus and spend it lavishly instead on barbecue and beer for the hunters, many of whom have never set foot inside a churchhouse door. The event will clear about $100, all said and done.

V. T. The initials won't stand for anything, but everyone will think they stand for "Very Tall." V. T. will be six-foot-five and wear his extra-long jeans tucked inside his high-heeled cowboy boots.

The "Boy" Thing

Sometimes Mama and Daddy just can't let go. In their minds, their son will always be their little boy, so they put the word "boy" on the end of his name. Permanently. You see these names in some redneck families: Eddieboy, Johnnyboy, Kennyboy, Pretty Boy, Babeboy. Kennyboy Tucker hasn't been a boy for seventy-five years, but he's still called Kennyboy. He's about eighty-five years old now, and the best catfisherman you'd ever want to know. He doesn't wear shoes because he's got calluses on his feet two inches thick from climbing riverbanks.

GIRLS

B. B. Sounds a little like "baby." If you choose to name her this, realize that even when she's eighty-two, her name is never going to sound like a grown-up's.

B. J. It'll stand for Betty Jo, Barbara Jo, Billie Jo, whatever. Think "Petticoat Junction," and abbreviate the sisters' names to initials. B. J. is the most popular initial-name for female rednecks.

C. C. Sounds like an emphatic "yes" in Spanish or the word "Sissy" spoken with a speech impediment.

J. C. Sounds kind of cute, like "Jacy." Also, the initials are appropriate for good Christians because they're the same as the Lord's initials.

J. J. Stands for "Jean Judy" but she'll never go by that; "J. J." sounds peppier anyway—a good thing because J. J.'s going to need all the pep she can get. She'll be a parole officer for juvenile offenders.

J. V. Short for junior varsity, the team she'll play basketball for.

K. C. Sounds cute and perky, like "Casey."

L. E. Sounds like "Ellie" with the last syllable drawn out.

P. D. Her real name will be Marie, but everyone will call her P. D., which stands for "pampered darling," and as an only child, she will live up to that name. Her husband will be known around town as P. W., though not to his face.

P. J. Probably stands for "Patti Jo," but "P. J." hints of pajamas and sounds more mysterious.

GIRLS WITH BOYISH NAMES

*G*irls are sometimes given boys' names, or boyish names, as a way to honor a male member of the family. Some say it's a subtle attempt to usurp male power in the traditional family. Whichever reason you choose to believe, rednecks do like to give their girls boys' names, but they often modify them with an *ette* or *ie* on the end. Sometimes they add a girl's name to a boy's name—Johnnie Mae, for example. All this transgenderism, though, doesn't work in reverse. Almost never do you see a boy named Sue. Redneck boys always get boys' names.

BO. A variation on the man's name, "Beau." Hey, it works for Bo Derek.

BOBETTE. Take Daddy's name, slap an *ette* on the end of it, and lil' ol' Bobette will have Daddy wrapped around her little finger for life. You can do this with a lot of daddies' names.

BRUCETTE. Not a very meticulous or detail-oriented person, she'll always have at least one couch or armchair with the springs and stuffing spilling out of it on her front porch.

CHARLENE. Feminine form of "Charles." She and her sisters Darlene and Nadine will all make a bundle of money selling Shaklee vitamin products. Rhyming all the children's names is important to some redneck families. (Charlene, Darlene, and Nadine Crump are cousins to Lloyd, Floyd, and Boyd Lyons.)

CHESTINE. Chester and Justine's girl will be flat as a pancake above the waist and have a syrupy-sweet personality.

CLYDA and **CLYDELLE.** Twin daughters of Clyde, who has a fairly large ego.

DANIELLE. Not only will her name remind everyone of Danielle Steele, author of steamy romance novels, but Danielle Sneltzer will hail from Climax, Georgia. She'll have a lot to live down before she even gets started in life.

EDWINA. Stylish, elegant Edwina will be the most popular singer at the annual Gospel Drag Show in Memphis. She'll style her hair in a flawless bubble 'do and wear a strapless midnight-blue cocktail dress and long black gloves. She and Jim Ed, who looks like a Lee Greenwood clone, will sing gospel duets with heartfelt sincerity, as they both attend church regularly. By day Edwina is known as Edwin and works as a chef downtown.

ERNESTINE. Female version of "Ernest," meaning exactly what it sounds like—"earnest, vigorous." Ernestine will be vigorous, all right. She'll hire a private detective and chase all around the country trying to find her sister Willene, to whom she loaned five dollars for gas. Willene put two dollars' worth in the tank, spent three dollars on the lottery, and won big time. Willene skipped town, and Ernestine will spend everything she has trying to find her. Figures Willene owes her big time.

FRANKIE LEE. A fly-fishing expert, she'll run a tiny shop for fly fishermen in Boise. Many men will try to charm her to get her to tell them where to find the best trout streams. Few will succeed.

GEORGEANNE. When a summer tornado rips the roof off her and Earl's house, he'll get to work the next day replacing it, but he'll get so hot working, he'll decide to cut off his long blond hair. Georgeanne will cut it for him, crying and sniffling a little, then braid it into a lock and put it in a special glass box with a little note that reads, "Earl's Tornado Hair." She'll display the box next to their treasured Z.Z. Top albums in the living room.

GERRILYNN. Jerry's daughter will have the unique ability to whistle like a man. This can look kinda funny sometimes when she's dressed up to go to town and standing by the car, and she puts two fingers in her mouth and whistles to Herman, who's in the house, to hurry up and come on.

GUYETTE. Feminine form of "Guy." If your baby's not a "Guy," have a "Guyette." Guyette will always have short dark hair, sparkling black eyes, be slightly masculine, and have an air of mystery about her. She'll attend Clemson University, spend her junior year abroad in Paris, and never return to the States.

JESSIE LOU. "Oh, my nerves!" will be her favorite expression. She'll always be a nervous sort, and when she gets especially shook up, her double chin will quiver, and that'll set her yippy little poodle, Poupette, to barking.

JIM. Some parents get a name set in their minds and decide to give their baby that name no matter what—whether it's a boy or a girl. Jim's parents did. Her name's not Jimmie Sue, not Jimmy Lou. Just Jim.

JO DAWN. Yep, your little darlin' was supposed to be a boy named Joe Don. Your cousin Wes the warlock predicted you were carrying a boy. You bought a lot of blue stuff. You got footballs for baby shower gifts. Then you had the prettiest little girl there ever was. You can still name her Joe Don, just spell it different.

JOELLA. The female form of "Joel," a Hebrew name meaning, "the Lord is willing." Joella is willing, too, and will go along with just about anything anyone suggests, so you need to be careful raising her because she'll wander off with anyone.

JOHNNIE MAE. An expert on greens, she'll raise a number of varieties organically on her small farm outside Atlanta and sell them to yuppie restaurants. Collard greens, turnip greens, tender greens, beet greens—if you cook 'em up separately and let her taste them in a blind taste test, she can tell you exactly what kind of green it is instantly. Her pickup is green and all the furniture in her house is green, too.

MARVINETTE. From the Old English name "Marvin," which means "famous friend." Marvinette will have a ski-slope nose just like her daddy and Bob Hope.

RANDI. She'll have a wild streak for a while like her boy-cousin Randy. Instead of manufacturing methamphetamines like Randy, though, she'll try to smuggle huge amounts of prescription narcotics such as Percodan, Demerol, and Dilaudid across the Rio Grande border into Texas. When the drug dogs nail her, she'll scream she has terminal cancer, but that won't melt the heart of the Border Patrol officer one whit.

Royalty

You can instill in children a sense of importance by giving them royalty or government officials' titles. Boys can be named Duke, Commodore, King, Senator, Governor, or Mayor. Girls can be named Queenie, Princess, or Duchess. These make good dogs' names too. Military-rank names are popular with some families. One redneck family named all its kids after military ranks: General, Colonel, Lieutenant, and Captain. The poor baby of the family was named Buck Private.

RAYMONDA. Female form of "Raymond." She'll raise yams for a living and be known as the Yam Lady. On Saturday mornings when yams are in season, she'll rise early, wash her hair, roll it with pink plastic curlers, and be down on the town square with her wagonload of yams, ready to do business by 8 A.M.

STEVETTE. A real sweet person, she'll enjoy her job as a grocery checkout clerk and call everybody "darlin'."

THOMASUE. This boy-girl combo name sounds kind of funny until you meet her, and then you'll think it's the most beautiful name in the world.

WILLENE. Her husband Willie Lee will win the lottery, but before they leave home in search of the perfect bass lake, Willene will take one last jab at her sister Ernestine, whom she can't stand. She'll send a terse note that reads, "Won $20 million. Kiss my ass."

BOYS ONLY

*R*eal boy-boy names borrowed from cowboys and the Old West.

BART. He'll love Western movies. His favorite will be *Tombstone*, and he'll like Val Kilmer as Doc Holliday the best.

BOONE. As in Daniel. Boone Koontz will take love of history back a few more centuries. He'll participate in English Renaissance fairs, wearing only a loincloth and bearskins. He'll drink lots of mead and carry a big roasted leg of mutton around for effect, letting the grease from it dribble onto his freckled beer belly.

CODY. Some girls are appropriating this name, too. Cody will raise a steer that'll win Grand Champion at his local Future Farmers of America Livestock Show.

COOT. Also known as Cooter or Cootie. Coot Higgins will wholeheartedly believe in the freedom to litter. Beer cans, old boots, monofilament fishing line—you name it, Coot tosses it out his pickup window with gleeful abandon. Road signs that announce a $500 fine for littering attract his special wrath: He peppers them with bullets from his .22 pistol. A sly old devil, he'll never get caught, either.

HOSS. After Hoss Cartright on *Bonanza*, the old TV series from the '60s. If you suspect your baby's not going to be at least six-foot-two and 250 pounds, consider another name.

SHANE. He'll be a decent man but conservative with his money. Old-timers will use an old country saying to describe him: "He's tighter than Dick's hatband."

SLADE. With his rancher friends, he'll build a shack on stilts down by the river and call it the Shack-a del Rio. It'll become a good-ol'-boy clubhouse of sorts, with no women allowed except on very special occasions. Every Friday night they'll cook a little barbecue or make chicken 'n' dumplings and sit around the fire and play poker. They'll talk politics, too, and decide who's going to become county judge or district attorney or, heck, president of the United States.

ZANE. After western author Zane Grey. Your Zane will dress in authentic 1880 cowboy clothes and participate in cowboy poetry contests throughout the western United States.

ZEKE. He'll wear a cowboy hat and have long hair that he'll wear in a braid down his back. Some of the older, more conservative rednecks in his mountain town will call him Zeke the Freak.

PLACE NAMES

*P*lace names are always good. Most people name their boys after places, but sometimes place names sound even better on girls.

BOYS

AUSTIN. He'll be a cowboy boot–wearin' computer geek who loves to water-ski.

DALLAS. He'll have social pretensions like certain Dallasites who are closet rednecks in denial. Dallas, whose family hails from Maypearl, Texas, will shun all vegetable dishes flavored with pork, turn up his nose at cornbread, and drive a Miata.

DENVER. He'll wear a sheepskin vest, have a long, droopy mustache, and squint his eyes a lot like Clint Eastwood.

ERIE and **HURON.** Great Lakes, great brothers' names, especially appropriate when their daddy's from Cleveland.

HOUSTON. Name your child after this town and he'll be big, friendly, easy-going, amenable to business, and about half-polluted all the time.

MACON. A perfectly wonderful town, but if you name your boy after it, expect a few schoolyard taunts, like kids calling him "Macon Bacon."

MONTANA. See Denver.

NEVADA. See Denver.

PARIS. After Paris, Texas, not the other Paris. Your son Paris will call up radio talk shows and rail against the Trilateral Commission, which he will perceive as the cause of his miseries.

RENO. Just Reno. He'll drop his last name, wear Buddy Holly nerd-glasses and a bolo tie, and be a hot, hot, hot jazz saxophone player.

GIRLS

ALABAMA. She'll be called "Allie" for short.

ASPEN. Aspenites hate it when rednecks (especially redneck Texans) name babies after their town. All the more reason to do it.

CHEYENNE. The preferred redneck spelling is "ShyAnn." There's nothing shy about her, though. She'll grow bored with her husband, Buck, who's always off hunting, and have an affair with Vernon, her ranch foreman. After about ten years, without a word of discussion, Buck will move out to his hunting camp, and Vernon will move into the big ranch house.

CLOVADALE. Just a made-up name, it sounds like a suburban subdivision in a southern town that drops its *R*s. Clovadale will rarely see her fisherman husband, but she will have a wry sense of humor and publish a cookbook of fifty catfish recipes called *Catfish on a Shingle*, the star recipe being a slab of catfish baked on a cedar plank for flavor.

GEORGIA. Her wiseacre boyfriend will always tell her, "I love you more than all the rented Mercedes in Atlanta."

IDALOU. Don't pronounce it "EYE-da-loo." It's "*AH*-da-loo," after the town in the Texas panhandle.

LOUISIANA. Choose this name with care. She'll let the good times roll, baby.

MEMPHIS. She'll be big and move slowly and make a modest living frying up Slugburgers at the Slugburger stand off Beale Street.

MIAMI. Pronounced "My-AM-*uh*," not "My-AM-ee." Miami Briggs will be a stripper in Dade County. She'll be so talented that the club owner she works for will even send her to Wisconsin for a special dancing and etiquette school for strippers.

SAVANNAH. She'll be as beautiful and sultry as the town she's named after.

SIERRA. Or Ciera, or Ciara. After a character on a popular TV soap opera. When she's a baby, the only way she'll be able to fall asleep for her nap in the afternoon is when the TV is tuned to a soap opera.

TARA. Name her after Scarlett's house and hope that she and Rhett can work things out.

TEXAS. Texas will shoot her husband Bubba in the thigh with a Smith & Wesson .38 while he's in bed with that slut Darlene. Bubba will drop charges, and, to make up, he and Texas will have another child.

Little and Big

Some rednecks give their sons and daughters the best name they know—their own. So to distinguish between father and son or mother and daughter, people have to use the prefixes "Little" and "Big." Big Ed, Little Ed. Big John, Little John. Big Reba, Little Reba. Big Dortha, Little Dortha. Rock Loggins decided to name his boy after himself; he and his boy are known as Big Rock and Little Rock.

TULSA. She'll attend Oral Roberts University.

UTAHNA. A Utah girls' name popular in the nineteenth century and resurrected for the twenty-first.

PEOPLE NAMED AFTER THINGS

Some rednecks name their kids after things because they think it's cute. Boys tend to be named after cars. With girls anything goes—from barbiturates to Barbie dolls.

BOYS

BRUT. Go ahead, name him after his daddy's aftershave.

BUICK. He'll be large and dependable, like the car he's named after.

BUTT-HEAD. Don't do it. Don't be tempted by your seven-year-old son's pleas to name his baby brother "Butt-head" after his favorite cartoon on TV, *Beavis and Butt-head.*

COTTON. When he's old, he'll have white hair and exhibit Puritanical tendencies. He'll write long, old-coot letters to the editor protesting taxes and the loss of morals in our culture. Think Cotton Mather. Think of his essay "What Must I Do to Be Saved?"

ELLIS U. For children of graduates of Louisiana State University. Ellis U. Oglesby always uses his middle initial, whether introducing himself at social occasions or signing a bill into law in the state legislature.

FLEETWOOD. If you think the name is from a Cadillac model or that mellow '70s rock group, you're wrong. Fleetwood's the name of a mobile home model (okay, trailer house), and that's exactly where he'll be conceived.

FORD. A good ol' all-American name. A good ol' All-American car. He's bound to be a good ol' all-American boy.

HARLEY. After Harley-Davidson motorcycles. Realize, of course, if you name him this and he joins the Hell's Angels, you preprogrammed him. Then again, he might join the Bikers for Christ and have a large cross tattooed on his chest. If you name him Harley, don't expect life to be normal.

GIRLS

BABY RUTH. Name her after your favorite candy bar. Baby Ruth's a better name than Butterfinger, which sounds almost gross, or Snickers, which sounds too preppy.

BAMBI. She should never marry a Buck. Other than that, she'll be all right. She'll probably teach twirling or cheerleading as a profession, after she retires from her job as a cheerleader for the Dallas Cowboys.

BARBI. Name her after the Barbie doll, but without the *e*, so it's not so obvious. If Barbi's a true redneck, she'll prefer G.I. Joe to Ken.

BRANDI. Or Brandee. Give her two sisters so you can name your daughters rhyming names—Brandee, Barbee, and Candee—and dress them in matching gingham dresses when they're little girls.

BUNNY. She'll be submissive, her nose will have a nervous tic, and she'll bear twelve children.

BUTIBEL. Butibel's mama, while pregnant and waiting in the doctor's office to see the doctor, will see an ad for a drug called "Butibel" in one of the doctor's magazines. "Hmm, Butibel," she'll think, her hormones swirling. "Why that's the prettiest name for a little girl I ever heard." And so that's how Butibel will come to be named for a possibly habit-forming barbiturate nerve pill.

CAMARO. Name her after the car she was conceived in. Classy, eh?

CANDI. When young, she'll sign her name with a heart over the *i*. When she's older and becomes a prosecutor for the district attorney's office, she'll change her name to Candace and conveniently forget that anyone ever, ever called her Candi.

CHABLIS. The Lady Chablis, an exuberant transvestite made famous in the book *Midnight in the Garden of Good and Evil*, pretty much owns this name. Chablis is fine, but for a more original wine/girl name, consider Chardonnay, Cabernet, or Merlot.

CHERRY JUNE. You could just name her Cherry, but giving her a double name offsets the bright, cheery (some might say fruity) effect of her first name. If your last name's Lewis, you can go for a rock 'n' roll vibe: Cherry Lee Lewis.

CHEVETTE. A small Chevy. If you're going to name someone after a car, why not name them after a breathtaking car? Say, a Duesenberg? Try it with a family name. Say, Duesenberg McClesky. Kinda has a ring to it.

DIMPLE. Make sure she has a dimple when she smiles. If people can't see the dimple, they'll wonder where it is. And she might show them.

DOVIE. She'll have white-white skin and light-blue eyes. A sensitive sort, she'll have agoraphobia and will very rarely go outside her and her husband Lamar's house. She'll wear only housecoats and terrycloth flip-flop houseshoes and survive on cigarettes, Dr. Pepper, and mayonnaise-and-white-bread sandwiches.

FAWN. Like Fawn Hall, Ollie North's secretary. Except Fawn Nicole Mabry won't be a secretary, she'll be a waitress at Hooter's where she'll serve up roasted chicken breasts with a wry smile.

HONEY. Do rednecks really name their daughters Honey? Yes. It can make for awkward business situations later, when she grows up and becomes a secretary and her married male boss asks her, in front of prospective clients at a business meeting, "Honey, could you hand me those sales projections?"

OLESTRA. Think about it: Would you really want to name your daughter after a fat substitute? When Fanny Fae Floyd was pregnant, she was reading a story in a ladies' magazine about olestra, a new fat substitute used in snack food, and she thought, "Olestra. Hmm, what a pretty name for a little girl."

TAMU. Should you name your daughter after your alma mater? Some Texas Aggies do. Tamu Crumpacker's parents named her after the university they attended: Texas A&M.

ABOUT THE AUTHOR

A former senior editor at *Houston Life* and *Houston Metropolitan* magazines, Linda Barth is an award-winning reporter now working as a freelance writer. She lives in Houston, Texas, but her ancestral home is Concrete, Texas, just across the river from Cheapside and down the road a bit from Cotton Patch.

Her special talents include Southern cooking, especially vegetables like cream peas and turnip greens. She can cook up a mean Dank gravy, as described in the book. She has honed her skill at changing tractor tires, which she has to do frequently on weekends when mowing over cactus and mesquite saplings on her family's farm near Concrete.

Writing *The Distinctive Book of Redneck Baby Names* involved special research to convey the story and colorful background that goes along with a good redneck name. She hung out at places where people tell good stories. One of her favorite places was a roadside cafe near Westhoff, Texas, where the waitress usually had a More cigarette dangling from her lips as she brought the fried chicken to the table. The folks at the Old Taylor Grocery outside Oxford, Mississippi, serve the best catfish on earth, along with charming tales of rural lives and loves. She also attended a Gospel Drag Show in Memphis and met a redneck "church lady" gospel singer who had the best bouffant hairdo seen since 1963. The ultimate source for information was a trip to Graceland.